The KING Is Coming

An Allegorical Tale for All and Sundry

written & illustrated
by

Blaine Turner

The KING Is Coming

Copyright © 2013

by

Blaine Turner

ISBN 978-0-578-12843-6

In this fast-paced allegory
the KING rides through a
wintry countryside to seek
his lost subjects. He sends
messengers ahead to prepare
the way—but one runs into
troubled hearts and a wicked
dragon. In humble cottages
this soldier discovers
something mystifying about
divine sovereignty and his
own free will. Would he be
able to survive the great
battle at the end? The story
comes complete with
quotations from The Holy
Scriptures.

Prologue

1   Dear Lover of God, this is for
2   you, an accurate account of a special
3   and life-giving KING who rules over
4   the blесséd land of Basileia.[1] In fact,
5   he not only rules the land and its
6   people, but he actually made them.[2]
7   That's why the ancients called him
8   the breath-giver.[3] So why do you
9   think he made all these people? Well
10 he did it to share his happiness with
11 them.[4] You see, he is good and kind,
12 and his people once loved him very
13 much. In fact they worshipped him.
14 They lived with him in the world's
15 grandest and most beautiful castle.[5]

---

[1] Basileia means "kingdom" in the Greek language.

[2] Genesis 1: [1]In the beginning God created the heavens and the earth. [27]So God created man in his own image, in the image of God he created him; male and female he created them.

[3] Genesis 2: [7]then the LORD God formed the man of dust from the ground and breathed into his nostrils the breath of life, and the man became a living creature.

[4] Psalm 16: [11]You make known to me the path of life; in your presence there is fullness of joy; at your right hand are pleasures forevermore.

[5] John 14: [2]In my Father's house are many rooms. If it were not so, would I have told you that I go to prepare a place for you?

16 It stands, even to this day atop a
17 majestic mountain covered in lush
18 green trees. Down below is a forest
19 teeming with lions and lizards and
20 wolves.[6] And one big flying dragon.[7]
21 But not to worry. The castle's stout
22 stone walls and battlements shine
23 like silver in the sunlight and its
24 many round towers are capped with
25 glistening copper and tin. Tall,
26 sinewy archers stand upon the
27 fortifications like so many mighty
28 angels, their bows ready, their
29 quivers quivering with arrows. If you
30 look closely, each seems to feign a
31 faint glow—some blue, some white,
32 some gold. They make a person feel
33 safe.[8]
34
35   Within these ramparts nests a
36 magnificent green garden
37 resplendent with all nature of flowers
38 and fruit, gorgeous and ripe for
39 gorging: pears, plums and of course
40 sweet, delicious apples. Small brooks

---

[6] Matthew 7: [15]Beware of false prophets, who come to you in sheep's clothing but inwardly are ravenous wolves.

[7] Revelation 12: [9]And the great dragon was thrown down, that ancient serpent, who is called the devil and Satan, the deceiver of the whole world— he was thrown down to the earth, and his angels were thrown down with him.

[8] Psalm 91: [11]For he will command his angels concerning you to guard you in all your ways.

41 and bunnies meander around tall
42 oaks and sycamores. Butterflies
43 ballet happily about and tickle the
44 dancing leaves with tiny toes. Sturdy
45 stone benches appear here and there
46 but sadly, now-a-days very few
47 people ever sit on them. In fact, of
48 the apparent 144,000[9] bedrooms in
49 the castle, only a mere twelve are
50 occupied. The rest, though cleaned
51 daily, remain like polished, but
52 empty shells on the beach.
53
54   You see, long ago almost all the
55 KING's subjects abandoned the
56 safety of the castle rooms and built
57 houses for themselves in the
58 countryside.[10] That might seem silly,
59 but they imagined a happier life
60 there. They craved adventure. They
61 longed for independence. They
62 wanted places of their own.[11] They
63 insisted on becoming their own
64 masters. For, can you believe it?
65 They started loving themselves more
66 than they loved their KING.[12] He was

---

[9] Revelation 14: [1]Then I looked, and behold, on Mount Zion stood the Lamb, and with him 144,000 who had his name and his Father's name written on their foreheads.

[10] Isaiah 53: [6a]All we like sheep have gone astray; we have turned—every one—to his own way;

[11] Matthew 6: [33]But seek first the kingdom of God and his righteousness, and all these things will be added to you.

[12] 2 Timothy 3: [2a]For people will be lovers

67 very sad about this, but let them go
68 nevertheless. Their worship had been
69 melody to his ears but he would not
70 force their affection. After all, you
71 cannot extract devotion from musical
72 instruments you must play yourself.
73
74   Quickly, however, their lives in
75 the countryside turned hard and
76 miserable. Winter came and never
77 went away.[13] Days became short and
78 nights long and cold. Their crops
79 burned with hoarfrost, causing
80 people to hunt for food and melt
81 snow for water. They were forced to
82 huddle in pathetic cabins around
83 pitiful cooking fires. At dusk they
84 shivered with thread-bare blankets
85 upon thin, straw mattresses. At dawn
86 the chamber pots beneath them were
87 frozen solid. Still, they didn't want to
88 return to the KING for fear he'd be
89 angry and make them toil as slaves.
90   So they made do and eventually
91 began to take some pleasure in their
92 way of life. They started calling
93 themselves the Pioneers. At least
94 they were living in liberty, they
95 began to remark. At least they were
96 free. At least they still had their
97 pride. Life, liberty and their personal

---

of self,
[13] Genesis 3: [17b]cursed is the ground because
of you; in pain you shall eat of it all the days
of your life

98   pursuits of happiness.[14] Liberté,
99   égalité, fraternité.[15]
100
101   Naturally they had children and
102   their children had children, and they
103   continued doing things their own
104   way.[16] They made up stories to mock
105   what they called the grandiose
106   mansion in the sky and the high-and-
107   mighty king inside. King? Some
108   even called him a myth, a make-
109   believe pretender to an imaginary
110   throne. A fairy tale. Others just
111   called him "the man upstairs" or "my
112   sky daddy." And another thing—to
113   their peril, they forgot all about the
114   dragon.
115
116   Eventually most people didn't
117   even believe there *was* a dragon, or a
118   king for that matter. Everyone
119   became his own king. Fights broke
120   out, as each person tried to get his
121   own way. Even the children
122   fought—boys with fists and girls
123   with pointing fingers, hurtful tongues
124   and stares. Some cowardly men tried
125   to pound women into servitude and
126   received only stone hearts for their
127   efforts. Fathers left families to find
128   fortunes which never materialized.

---

[14] From the United States Declaration of
Independence
[15] The national motto of France
[16] Judges 17: [6b]Everyone did what was right
in his own eyes.

129 Mothers lured strange men home to
130 replace them, only to be disappointed
131 repeatedly. Sons went off to war and
132 shed blood, while nubile daughters
133 wandered late at night and shed
134 tears.
135
136   In spite of this, as years passed,
137 the real KING never forgot his
138 people. He loved them[17]—wept for
139 them[18]—did not want any of them to
140 perish.[19] So one day he decided to
141 ride out and visit them.[20]
142   Accordingly he sent ahead
143 several messengers to prepare the
144 way.[21] Some were short, some tall,
145 some gallant, some talented,

---

[17] Psalm 136: [26]Give thanks to the God of
heaven, for his steadfast love endures
forever.
[18] Luke 19: [41]And when he drew near and
saw the city, he wept over it, [42]saying,
"Would that you, even you, had known on
this day the things that make for peace! But
now they are hidden from your eyes.
[19] Ezek. 33: [11]Say to them, 'As surely as I
live, declares the Sovereign Lord, I take no
pleasure in the death of the wicked, but
rather that they turn from their ways and
live. Turn! Turn from your evil ways! Why
will you die, people of Israel?'
[20]Revelation 3: [20]Behold, I stand at the door
and knock. If anyone hears my voice and
opens the door, I will come in to him and eat
with him, and he with me.
[21] 2 Corinthians 5: [20]Therefore, we are
ambassadors for Christ, God making his
appeal through us. We implore you on
behalf of Christ, be reconciled to God.

146 others—well; here is the story of
147 one.

The KING Is Coming

Part One

Once upon a wintry afternoon by
a white and winding trail there stood
a tiny wooden shack called Safenook
Lodge. It was customary to name
every inhabited house, no matter
how humble. This one had a quaint
straw-thatched roof, thick and
heavily laden with snow. The home
was cozy-looking—inviting with its
yellow, fire-lit windows and lazy
smoke drifting from a rustic
fieldstone chimney. Deep snow-
drifts had been cleared from the trail
but the approaching horse hooves
still kicked up fairy-dust flakes and
engraved curved prints in the freshly
fallen crystals.

A mysterious black-clad rider
swung from his saddle and tied his
silver steed to a hitching post.
Adjusting a gleaming sword by his
side, he stamped up four steps to the
landing and banged heavily upon the
front door. A wee pixie lass
answered, gazing all the while at his
magnificent, shiny riding boots.

"Little Lily Charity at yer
service," she said, curtsying

178 awkwardly and forgetting that her
179 father had warned never to give her
180 name or dragon-tax number to
181 strangers. She had short brown curls,
182 like karakul and growing as moss on
183 a rock. Her dark brown eyes were set
184 narrow and aloof. Her nose was
185 pinched playfully, her lips thin and
186 pouty. Her figure seemed slender but
187 shapely—almost fetching. Tiny
188 hands folded delicate fingers neatly
189 across a coarse cotton smock.
190   "Is the man of the house at
191 home?" the messenger demanded,
192 wrinkling his eyebrows at her hair.
193   "My father's out huntin in dem
194 woods of arn," came the very small
195 voice in reply. The messenger
196 continued to stare. She winced. "He
197 shaved me skull cuz uh duh lice,
198 okay," she said, cocking her head
199 and frowning up into his face. "I dun
200 suppose yuh gots lice up dare where
201 yuh live."
202   Undaunted, the man burst past
203 her into the cottage, slammed the
204 door on the swirling snow and
205 bellowed into her shocked face,
206 "Then I will talk to the mistress of
207 the home. It is a matter of most
208 urgency. The KING is coming[22] and
209 you must receive him."[23] The man's

---

[22] John 12: [15b]your king is coming
[23] Colossians 2: [6]Therefore, as you received
Christ Jesus the Lord, so walk in him,

210 large and looming presence made the
211 tiny shack seem even smaller.
212   "But uh gots no mistress,
213 monsignor sir, no mudda uh any
214 sort," the small voice quavered this
215 time. "I be dee only lady uh dis
216 lowly dwelling. Though some day I
217 would love tuh have Raspille, me
218 dashing make-believe desperado—
219 sweep me far away from dis dung-
220 dirty wattle and daub."²⁴ She leaned
221 hard against the wall.
222   "Nonsense! You are too young
223 to be swept away!" the messenger
224 roared, but on further glance noticed
225 she was no mere child either.
226   "The KING is on tour from his
227 castle on Steeplechase Mountain," he
228 continued. "Along the way he has
229 decreed to have wine and bread with
230 his subjects—so they might
231 remember The Good Times. He has
232 chosen to partake next at this very
233 spot. He rides where he will, you
234 know; and chooses whom he will.
235 He is the KING. You are commanded
236 to receive him and serve table within
237 the hour! You are a chosen one, he
238 has ordained it."²⁵

---

²⁴ "wattle and daub" is strips of wood woven
together then covered in a plaster of animal
hair and clay
²⁵ Ephesians 1: ⁴he chose us in him before
the foundation of the world, that we should
be holy and blameless before him.

239   "Lordy be," said Charity,
240   suddenly standing erect. "Rye buns I
241   got sir but, with acorns baked in
242   see—pretty crappy service for duh
243   likes of your own royal selves."
244   "Don't be impudent, little one,"
245   the soldier rasped, "May I call you
246   Lily? I see you have a table and two
247   stools. Surely you have cupcakes, or
248   at least a nice crumpet or two for
249   your Lord."
250   "Cupcakes?" she whined, "do
251   yuh think me gots time to bake king-
252   fancy sweet-cakes out here in duh
253   freakin boondocks?" She threw up
254   her hands and then clasped them
255   behind her back. Turning away
256   slightly she said, "You ken call me
257   Lily if yer a mind to; lily white
258   means dat every soul becomes
259   innocent 'gen when they die. Pretty
260   good trick, huh? Fer duh likes uh
261   me." She blushed. "But are ya
262   thinkin we idle away our earthly
263   days makin bonbons? There's a last
264   bowl of garlic berry pottage for ya
265   and a leftover rabbit leg maybe. We
266   really got nuttin here fit fer a bleedin
267   powder-wig king."
268   Scratching his head, the man
269   rose to his most imposing height and
270   growled over her, "You crude
271   hunters! Have you no proper food?"
272   "As uh told yuh befoe, yo
273   Reverence," came the shy but plucky
274   reply, "we got nuttin; me pa has went

275 huntin. We ain't got time fuh wine
276 parties!"
277   "Save that excuse for the KING,"
278 stammered the messenger, "for
279 you'll need it. Don't you know what
280 he does to those who spurn him
281 thus? Choose for yourself today
282 whom you will serve: your
283 Sovereign Lord or your own pitiful
284 selfishness."[26]
285   The man leaned imposingly over
286 the tiny girl and small pearls of
287 perspiration appeared on her
288 forehead. But sweat appeared on his
289 own brow as well, for he imagined
290 how the KING could make life
291 unbearable, not only for those who
292 repulse his advances or seek to
293 thwart his will, but also for his
294 servants who fail to perform. And
295 surely, he pondered, it would not
296 please if his missionary failed to win
297 the wayward subjects.
298   Suddenly a tear appeared in one
299 of the girl's narrow brown eyes.
300 Then another slid down her pale
301 cheek to fall upon a tiny bare foot.
302 "Your Imminence, truly we got no fit
303 food fer a king's wine party—we got
304 so little of anything, so little of
305 everything. It's a hectic time fer us."
306   "Well I can see that, peasant,"
307 the soldier spat disgustedly; "he's

---

[26] Joshua 24: [15b]choose this day whom you
will serve

308 coming nevertheless. Perhaps I could
309 offer you to him as a slave girl. You
310 know how to bow and scrub floors, I
311 assume. And light his candles when
312 it gets dark?"
313   With this, the girl crumpled into
314 a heap of bones on the floor and
315 began to sob heavily, but as quietly
316 as she could manage. Eventually, she
317 was able to pick herself up and with
318 a streaked face, look squarely into
319 that of the harsh messenger.
320   "Yessah, Yer Pontification," she
321 said evenly through gaunt, almost
322 lifeless lips. "I'm a peasant so I'm
323 cool at scrubbing floors, and even
324 cleaning windows—but I will not
325 bow, not even a little. Uh do not
326 want tuh serve yuh stupid king. Even
327 if he be strong and handsome. He
328 ain't mine. He lives far, far away.
329 You ken take muh possessions, take
330 muh freedom, take muh body, muh
331 spirit, take even muh life. Then you
332 will have a dead corpse. But you will
333 never have me free will. I ain't yer
334 barnyard animal."[27]
335   The soldier stared deeply into
336 her sad, slit-like eyes. She held him

---

[27] Genesis 1: [26]Then God said, "Let us make
man in our image, after our likeness. And let
them have dominion over the fish of the sea
and over the birds of the heavens and over
the livestock and over all the earth and over
every creeping thing that creeps on the
earth."

337 transfixed while her mournful gaze
338 tried to penetrate his ironclad heart.
339   "Small one," he asked, "why
340 would you let a lack of the finer
341 things keep you from your KING, and
342 thwart his sovereign will? He doesn't
343 care about them! He knows your life
344 is hard. So hasn't he stated his will
345 that all should come to him?[28] And
346 hasn't he commanded you to take his
347 yoke upon you, and learn from
348 him?"[29]
349   "But I'm just a piece uh bull-
350 crap," came the reply from a now
351 lifeless face, "What? Add his yoke,
352 whatever it is, to me workload? I
353 don't think so. Tell him tuh look fer
354 his bread 'n wine elsewhere! Ah
355 can't give him a crumb or a sip."
356   "But he has ordained it!" said
357 the messenger with a puzzled look.[30]

---

[28] 2 Peter 3: [9]The Lord is not slow to fulfill his promise as some count slowness, but is patient toward you, not wishing that any should perish, but that all should reach repentance.

[29] Matthew 11: [28]Come to me, all who labor and are heavy laden, and I will give you rest. [29]Take my yoke upon you, and learn from me, for I am gentle and lowly in heart, and you will find rest for your souls. [30]For my yoke is easy, and my burden is light."

[30] Romans 8: [28]And we know that for those who love God all things work together for good, for those who are called according to his purpose. [29]For those whom he foreknew he also predestined to be conformed to the image of his Son, in order that he might be

358
359   Just then outside there was a
360 thundering through the forest and a
361 wild galloping of horses, nostrils
362 flaring, breaths visible in great
363 bellows. Snow from tree-branches,
364 jarred loose by the tumult, descended
365 in great clumps to the trail below.
366 Through them came none other than
367 the KING himself, bounding in bright
368 purple garments and with a great
369 gold riding-crown in his hair. He
370 rode right up to the door of the
371 cottage and stopped suddenly amidst
372 a flurry of flowing robes and sashes.
373 Immediately, the messenger burst
374 out to greet him on the snow glazed
375 landing.
376   "Sovereign Lord," he said,
377 bowing as low as possible in
378 leotards, "the poor soul inside, being
379 vulgar in speech, feeble in mind and
380 hard of heart has, in spite of my best
381 labors, willfully and maliciously
382 refused to accept Your Grace,[31] even
383 though you must clearly have
384 ordained otherwise! Else why would
385 you have sent me here to bid her
386 prepare table?"[32]

---

the firstborn among many brothers.

[31] John 5: [40]yet you refuse to come to me
that you may have life.

[32] Matthew 28: [19]Go therefore and make
disciples of all nations, baptizing them in the
name of the Father and of the Son and of the
Holy Spirit, [20]teaching them to observe all

387   The KING replied slowly in a
388   fatherly tone, "Be not so anxious,
389   prickly one. We decree that she will
390   not accept us because, while she may
391   appear very humble, she is in fact
392   filled with a stubborn pride nature
393   and is incapable of accepting us.[33]
394   We decree thus, for we are in full
395   control,[34] but at the same time we
396   afford her complete and genuine
397   choice in the matter. We do not
398   manipulate puppets. Yes, we have
399   given her the free will to accept or
400   reject us. We do not desire the fealty
401   of marionettes. So she chooses for
402   herself, and as a result she is fully
403   responsible for her actions. She loves
404   her material things, humble as they
405   are, more than her Lord-creator.
406   Sadly, her unfortunate decision will
407   lead to her death.[35] It makes us very
408   sad.[36] But she must get what she
409   deserves because we are just."[37]

---

that I have commanded you. And behold, I
am with you always, to the end of the age.
[33] Ephesians 2: [1]And you were dead in the
trespasses and sins
[34] 1 Corinthians 4: [20]For the kingdom of God
does not consist in talk but in power.
[35] John 3: [36]Whoever believes in the Son has
eternal life; whoever does not obey the Son
shall not see life, but the wrath of God
remains on him.
[36] Ezekiel 33: [11a]Say to them, As I live,
declares the Lord GOD, I have no pleasure
in the death of the wicked, but that the
wicked turn from his way and live; turn
back, turn back from your evil ways

410   "Is that fair?" the messenger
411 dared to ask. "She is so hauntingly
412 beautiful."
413   "Fair? Haunting? Are not my
414 ways higher than your ways?"
415 demanded the KING, giving his
416 messenger a penetrating stare. "And
417 is not my understanding above your
418 understanding?[38] Did you create the
419 heavens and the earth? Did you set
420 the sun in its path, or even the snow
421 on this trail?[39] Now you see the light
422 as if wandering in a forest. Later you
423 will walk in the open meadow."[40]
424   With this, the KING stroked his
425 long beard and brushed snow out of
426 it. Then he blinked a tear out of his
427 eye, turned his horse, and called over
428 his shoulder. "Yeoman servant," he
429 said, "shake the snow off your feet,[41]
430 ride ahead, swiftly away to the next

---

[37] Revelation 16: [7]And I heard the altar saying, "Yes, Lord God the Almighty, true and just are your judgments!"

[38] Isaiah 55: [9]For as the heavens are higher than the earth, so are my ways higher than your ways and my thoughts than your thoughts.

[39] Job 28: [4]"Where were you when I laid the foundation of the earth?

[40] 1 Corinthians 13: [12]For now we see in a mirror dimly, but then face to face. Now I know in part; then I shall know fully, even as I have been fully known.

[41] Mark 6: [11]And if any place will not receive you and they will not listen to you, when you leave, shake off the dust that is on your feet as a testimony against them.

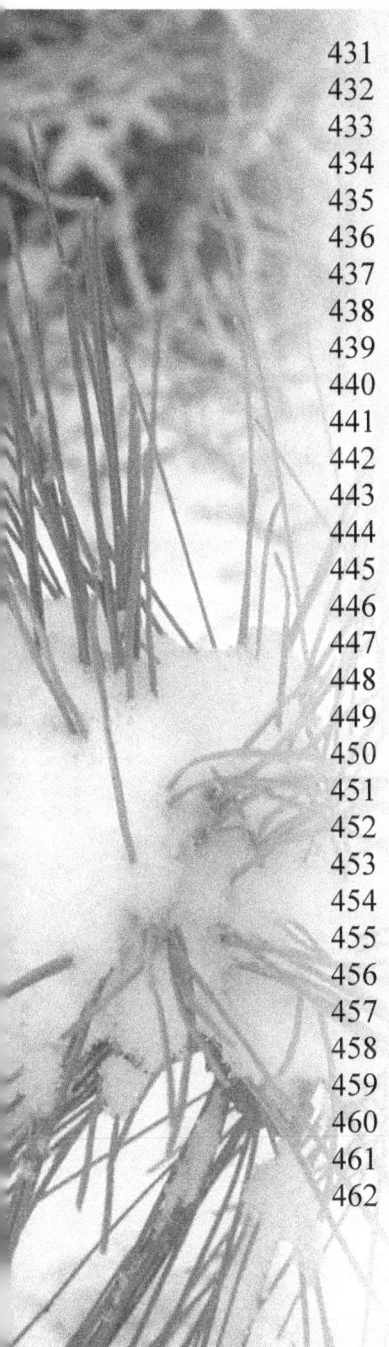

431 village and arrange a proper table
432 with someone else. Someone I will
433 again show you. Make haste. Tell
434 them the KING is coming."[42]
435   Then the KING stopped short
436 and bade the girl approach. She
437 stood dwarfed by the thigh of his
438 mighty steed—massive muscle
439 twitching by the light stroke of
440 maiden garments loose in the breeze.
441 Bending from his saddle, the KING
442 spoke softly. "Charity, did my
443 messenger give you anything?"
444   "No, Suh," she replied,
445 trembling.
446   He immediately leaned down to
447 hand her something. Hesitant but
448 curious, she grasped it with small
449 fingers. "I have written you a
450 personal letter," the KING said, "and
451 many are martyred to deliver it. I
452 hope you understand. Two pages in
453 every three describe the KING and
454 his mighty deeds. One page informs
455 how to respond in worship through
456 His power. Take care not to self-
457 centeredly dwell on the one, thereby
458 neglecting the two, which have co-
459 requisite meaning."
460   Later, from her window, and
461 with the fire-glow behind her, the
462 haunting, thin girl watched the two

---

[42] Matthew 16: [28]Truly, I say to you, there
are some standing here who will not taste
death until they see the Son of Man coming
in his kingdom.

463 figures depart down the snowy trail.
464 Then, with a sigh of relief, she tossed
465 the "letter" over by the firewood (it
466 was a whole book!) and began
467 preparations to serve dinner to her
468 beloved father. He would be
469 returning soon from hunting.
470   "Yuh just can't really trust
471 kings," she muttered, "or their magic
472 books, and fancy, sword carrying
473 messengers!" How adorable and
474 grownup she looked, setting the table
475 with all kinds of goodies which had
476 been hidden away in the pantry.
477
478   But at that moment the dragon,
479 not her father, was hovering at her
480 door—and his appetite was
481 considerably greater than a few small
482 goodie-cakes.[43] And he had her
483 dragon-tax number tight in his fist.

---

[43] 1 Peter 5: [8]Be sober-minded; be watchful.
Your adversary the devil prowls around like
a roaring lion, seeking someone to devour.

Part Two

485

486   Further along the white and
487 winding trail the messenger ventured
488 upon a second abode, a tiny log
489 cabin called Stoutnest Manor. It had
490 a charming wood-shake roof, rough
491 and partly blanketed with snow. It
492 was snug and inviting with its
493 yellow, fire-flecked windows and
494 lively smoke billowing from a
495 stubby rock chimney. The deep
496 snow-drifts had been shoveled from
497 the path but the approaching hooves
498 still tossed up tiny flecks that danced
499 magically around the furiously
500 churning horse legs.
501   Directly, the horseman tied his
502 steed to a post and tucking his sword
503 under his cape, tromped up the steps
504 to rap piercingly on the front door. A
505 little poppet named Tulip Hope
506 answered, gazing all the while with
507 round green eyes at his oversized,
508 solid-silver belt buckle. She had long
509 eyelashes, black ringlets cascading
510 down her back and a button nose
511 turned up impishly. Her lips were
512 full and round like her body. Stubby
513 fingers folded themselves nervously
514 across her neatly pressed linen
515 smock.
516   "Is the man of the house at
517 hand?" the soldier enquired
518 wrinkling his forehead.

519   "Mine father is tending sheep in
520 the fields by day," came a mellow
521 voice in reply.
522   Unperturbed, the man pushed
523 into the cottage, shut the door on the
524 swirling snow and growled through
525 clenched teeth into her astonished
526 face, "Then I will talk with the
527 mistress of the house. It is a matter
528 of most urgency. The KING is
529 coming and you must accept him."
530   "But I have no mistress, no
531 mother at all, sir," came the soft
532 voice again, quavering this time, "I
533 am the only lady of this humble
534 abode, although someday soon I
535 should like to be the Lady of a rich
536 and noble Lord. I may not be worthy
537 of him but my name is Tulip, which
538 in white means forgiveness."
539   "Fiddlesticks!" the messenger
540 barked. "You are too miniature to be
541 a lady! You are alone, girl? The
542 KING is on tour from his castle on
543 Steeplechase. Along the way he has
544 decreed to have refreshments with
545 his subjects. He has chosen to
546 partake next at this very spot. He
547 rides where he will, and chooses
548 whom he will. He is the KING. You
549 are ordered to accept him and set
550 your table within the hour! You are a
551 chosen one, he has foreseen it."
552   "Sir," Hope said, "I have but
553 nary a pot of cabbage nut mush and
554 some brambleberry ale. It would be

555 so nice if thy king could bring along
556 some Rhine wine for us. Or
557 something from France or Spain. We
558 are so unfortunate here and
559 deserving. Also some nice pewter
560 goblets to drink it from and some
561 delicate jelly rolls to serve beside it.
562 And Russian tea cakes. On gold
563 rimmed plates, of course. Fit for a
564 king. Oh, I'm sure he's the answer to
565 all mine hopes. Is he married, by the
566 way?"
567   "Don't be insolent, little miss,"
568 hissed the man, "I see you have a
569 table and three stools. Surely you
570 have meat, or at least a pond fish or
571 two ready for your Lord."
572   "There's a last bit of shepherd's
573 goulash and a leftover pig's foot,"
574 she pouted. "I feel so mortified that
575 my table's not fit for thee or thy
576 royalty. It's been a bad year. It's
577 always winter and I go crazy all
578 cooped up in these four log walls.
579 Yes, tell thy king we need another
580 stool as well. Or better yet a chair. It
581 was so cold the other night I used
582 one for firewood." The maiden
583 shivered and folded her arms about
584 herself.
585   Not impressed, the man puffed
586 out his chest and snarled over her,
587 "You simple shepherds! You have
588 fields full of sheep but no lamb in the
589 larder?"

590   "Larder?" came the brusque
591   reply, "as I told thy Righteousness,
592   the cupboard is bare. My father is
593   always out tending his flock. He has
594   no time for this house or me. No
595   wonder I'm so poor and messed up.
596   But thy king can bestow on me
597   everything I should ever need."
598   The messenger sputtered.
599   "Young lady, the KING is not a Santa
600   Claus or Prince Charming. Surely
601   you know that he is more than a
602   social worker or even a miracle
603   worker. Choose for yourself today
604   whom you will serve: the Sovereign
605   Lord of your life or a candy man for
606   your lips."
607   The messenger leaned
608   commandingly over the cowering
609   girl and small gems of perspiration
610   appeared on her forehead. But sweat
611   also appeared on his brow, for he
612   pictured how the KING could surely
613   make life arduous, not only for those
614   who refuse his Lordship—but also
615   for his missionaries who fail to
616   properly explain what it means to
617   have refreshments with the KING.
618   Suddenly a tear appeared in one
619   of the girl's beautiful green eyes.
620   Then another slid down her ruddy,
621   round cheek to moisten a tiny
622   stockinged foot. "Thy Magnification,
623   truly I am totally distraught by my
624   rotten life. Okay, forget about giving
625   me presents. Never mind that I am

626 less fortunate than thee. But I would
627 so appreciate the king giving me a
628 hand out of this tormented existence.
629 I'm coming to him on my knees!"
630 "The KING is not your royal
631 benefactor, flea-brain," the
632 messenger hissed dejectedly, "He's
633 coming for a higher reason. Perhaps
634 I could offer you as a servant girl.
635 You know how to curtsy and mop
636 floors, I presume. And light his fires
637 in the evening?"
638 With this, Hope fell limply to
639 the floor in a blob and began to cry
640 softly. Eventually though, she was
641 able to pick herself up and with
642 moistened eyes, look squarely into
643 those of the stern soldier.
644 "Yea," she said frigidly, "I'm
645 able to scrub, but I will never curtsy,
646 not now, not ever. I don't want to
647 serve thy pointless king. He's not my
648 thing. I don't have the time anyway.
649 I'm way too busy. What has he ever
650 done for me? Okay take my
651 possessions, take my freedom, take
652 my innocence, my spirit, take even
653 my life. Then you will have a stiff,
654 dead body. But you will never have
655 my free will. I am not your stuffed
656 doll."
657 The messenger stared deeply
658 into her oval, steadfast eyes. She
659 held him fixed until her determined
660 gaze sank deep and began to
661 permeate his armored heart.

662   "Captivating one," he breathed,
663 "why would you let your love of
664 possessions keep you from the most
665 precious treasure ever? You thwart
666 his sovereign will. For hasn't he
667 stated his pleasure that all should
668 come to him?[44] And isn't it written
669 that he stands at your door and
670 knocks? All you have is but to open
671 it and have a bite with him."[45]
672   "But I simply refuse," came the
673 reply from pursed, red lips. This is a
674 hectic time for me. I just can't fit in
675 another commitment! It's not worth
676 my while."
677   "But he has ordained it!" said
678 the messenger with an exasperated
679 look.
680
681   Just then, outside there was a
682 crashing through the forest and a
683 frightful galloping of hooves, flaring
684 nostrils, and breaths visible in
685 billowy clouds. Snow from sagging
686 tree-branches, jarred loose by the
687 turmoil, fell away in giant clumps to
688 the trail below. Through them burst
689 the KING galloping in gorgeous

---

[44] Isaiah 1: [18] "Come now, let us reason together, says the Lord: though your sins are like scarlet, they shall be as white as snow; though they are red like crimson, they shall become like wool.
[45] Revelation 3: [20]Behold, I stand at the door and knock. If anyone hears my voice and opens the door, I will come in to him and eat with him, and he with me.

690 purple garments and a great golden
691 riding-crown. He rode directly up to
692 the door of the cabin and stopped
693 abruptly amidst a flurry of flowing
694 cloaks and mantles. Directly, the
695 messenger popped out to salute him
696 on the snow encrusted landing.
697   "Your Majesty," he said,
698 bowing as low as possible with a
699 sword under his cape, "the pitiable
700 soul inside, being twisted in mind
701 and stubborn of heart, has despite my
702 efforts, willfully refused to accept
703 Your Grace, even though you must
704 have foreseen otherwise! For you are
705 all-knowing. So why would you have
706 sent me here to have her prepare
707 table?"
708   The KING replied, "We knew
709 that she would not accept us now
710 because, while she may appear very
711 busy, she is actually totally self-
712 absorbed and prideful about her
713 meaningless activity and empty
714 accomplishments. She seeks only a
715 means to worldly peace and
716 prosperity.[46] Nevertheless, she is free
717 to accept us if she so chooses.
718 Everyone is. We do not seek
719 devotion from toy dollies. We give
720 her complete and genuine free will in

---

[46] Matthew 6: [24]"No one can serve two
masters, for either he will hate the one and
love the other, or he will be devoted to the
one and despise the other. You cannot serve
God and money.

721 the matter of choice. As a result she
722 is fully responsible for her actions
723 and in her case, will obtain the
724 ensuing consequences. Yes, we
725 know beforehand what the decision
726 of her heart is. We are KING. And
727 yes, we control even her heart, but
728 nevertheless she also is master of her
729 fate."
730   "Is that just?" the messenger
731 was bold to ask. "She is so young
732 and beautiful."
733   "Just? Young? Beautiful? My
734 ways are above your ways," said the
735 KING patiently, "and my
736 understanding is more excellent than
737 your understanding. For now you see
738 the truth as if cowering in a cave.
739 Later you will stand on the mountain
740 top."
741   With this, the KING stroked his
742 long beard and brushed snow out of
743 it. Then with the hint of a smile, he
744 turned his horse, and called over his
745 shoulder. "Well-meaning and faithful
746 steward," he said, "shake the snow
747 off your feet, ride ahead, swiftly
748 away to the next village and arrange
749 a proper visit with yet someone else.
750 Someone I will again show you.
751 Make haste. Tell them the KING is
752 coming."[47]

---

[47] Matthew 21: [5]"Say to the daughter of
Zion, 'Behold, your king is coming to you,
humble, and mounted on a donkey, on a
colt, the foal of a beast of burden.'"

753
754   Then the KING commanded the
755 girl to approach. She obeyed and
756 stood dwarfed by the massive neck
757 of his mighty steed. Her long hair
758 wafted up to mingle with the edges
759 of its mane. The KING addressed her
760 kindly, "Hope, did my messenger
761 offer you anything?"
762   "No, Master," she replied, her
763 voice quavering.
764   He immediately leaned down
765 and handed her a book. Startled, she
766 gripped it lightly in her short fingers.
767 "I have written you a personal
768 letter," he said, "and many people
769 have sacrificed their lives to deliver
770 it in your own language. I hope you
771 understand. Two thirds describes
772 who I am and one third tells how to
773 respond in worship through my
774 power. Take care against self-
775 centered focus on human response,
776 missing deep appreciation of the
777 Royal Nature. Ask not what your
778 KING can do for you, and not even
779 what you can do for your KING but
780 rather ask who you can be for your
781 KING. From living for me stems
782 suitable service and seemly
783 supplication."
784
785   From her window, and
786 silhouetted in the fire-glow, the
787 beautiful young maiden watched the
788 two riders depart down the snowy

789 trail. Then, with a sigh of relief, she
790 tucked the book in a cabinet and
791 began hasty preparations to set table
792 for her father's return from sheep
793 tending. "I just really don't have
794 time for kings," she mused, "and
795 their pompous, cape-waving
796 messengers! They're full of empty
797 promises and only breed false hopes.
798 I'm fully capable of discerning my
799 own priorities. Someday if I should
800 ever have spare time, I might glance
801 at that book of his. But it looks so
802 long."
803   While she was waiting for her
804 father, she lay down from her hectic
805 life for a nice winter's nap. Her
806 weary body melted pleasurably into
807 her fluffy feather bed. She dreamed
808 in vivid detail of her golden prince of
809 peace who she prayed would soon
810 come save her with a kiss. A
811 sentiment to be relished, returned
812 and remain on her full lips forever.
813 This was her dearest hope.
814
815   But the red dragon[48], ravenous
816 and venomous, not a gilded prince
817 was just then preying at her door.
818 And his kiss could be all-consuming.

---

[48] Revelation 12: [3]And another sign
appeared in heaven: behold, a great red
dragon, with seven heads and ten horns, and
on his heads seven diadems.

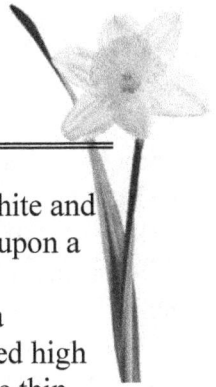

Part Three

820

821   Still further along the white and
822 winding trail the rider came upon a
823 tiny terracotta cottage called
824 Honeysuckle Haven. It had a
825 picturesque clay tile roof piled high
826 with snow, and ice coated the thin
827 dead vines climbing its sides. It was
828 cozy, inviting with yellow fire-
829 etched windows and sweet, wild
830 cherry smoke wafting from a tall red-
831 brick chimney. The deep snow-drifts
832 had been carefully cleared from the
833 walkway suggesting a diligent and
834 prudent occupant. The approaching
835 horse stirred up crystals like fairy-
836 dust which clung to its legs as stately
837 white dress socks.
838   The rider approached and tied
839 his mount to a post. He left his sword
840 on the saddle and trundled up the
841 steps to tap tentatively on the front
842 door. He was sad that people were
843 not responding to him by accepting
844 the Lord. Maybe he was being too
845 harsh. Maybe it was his black
846 clothes, white collar or fancy ring.
847 Maybe it was his self-assured,
848 superior manner. Well after all, he
849 was the only one with the truth; all
850 the peasants were ignorant and
851 warped in their thinking. Never-
852 theless, he vowed to try and act more
853 like the KING he represented. He
854 knocked again.

855   A diminutive damsel dubbed
856 Faith Daffodil answered—gazing all
857 the while at his fancy white collar.
858 The daffodil, by the way symbolizes
859 spring, rebirth and new beginnings.
860 The girl had long blond hair falling
861 straight about her slim shoulders, an
862 innocent, fresh face, and graceful
863 long fingers folded across a stiff,
864 sundried white smock.
865   "Is the man of the house at
866 home?" the messenger asked,
867 wringing his hands.
868   "My poor father lost his
869 faculties years ago," said the steady
870 voice in response, "and now spends
871 all his time in the back room staring
872 out the window. He loves to talk
873 about silky birds and shiny snow, but
874 he doesn't even remember my
875 name."
876   Saddened, the man slipped into
877 the cottage, closed the door on the
878 snarling snow and whispered into the
879 small, somber face, "Then I will
880 speak with the mistress of the house,
881 if you please. It's a matter of extreme
882 urgency. The KING is coming and
883 would very much like you to invite
884 him in."
885   "But there is no mistress here
886 kind sir," the girl replied from
887 trembling red lips. "Mother was
888 killed by a forest beast. I am the only
889 lady of this tiny abode, although

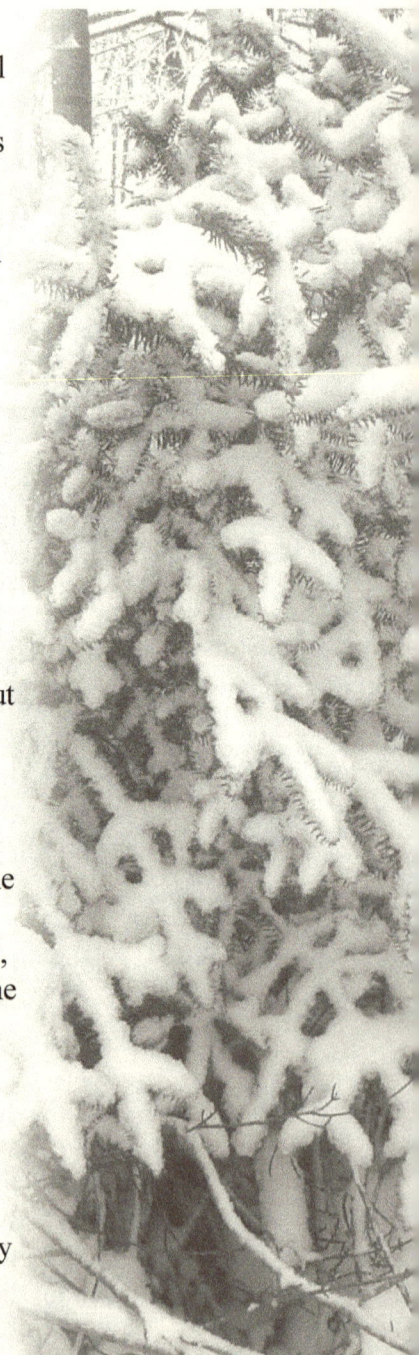

890 some day I should like to reach the
891 ends of the earth."[49]
892   "You are here with your father
893 alone?" the messenger asked. "The
894 KING is on tour from his castle.
895 Along the way he has decreed that he
896 shall visit with his subjects. He has
897 chosen to partake next at this very
898 spot. He rides where he will, you
899 know and chooses whom he will. He
900 is the KING. You are invited to ask
901 him in and serve refreshments within
902 the hour! Do you have sugar plums
903 and mead? [50] You are the chosen
904 one, he has predestined it."
905   "Refreshments?" asked the girl.
906 "Even mead, sir, is way too dear, but
907 I have some old barley ale. And will
908 my almighty King settle for mere
909 crusts of beechbran bread and
910 bumble pie?"
911   "Don't be sassy, silly girl," the
912 messenger tried not to grumble, "I
913 see you have a table and four stools.
914 Surely you have plumb pudding, or
915 at least a sweet-candy or two for
916 your Lord."

---

[49] Acts 1: [8]But you will receive power when
the Holy Spirit has come upon you, and you
will be my witnesses in Jerusalem and in all
Judea and Samaria, and to the end of the
earth.
[50] Mead is an alcoholic beverage, made from
honey and water by fermentation with yeast.

917   "There is a last crock of
918 buckbeet pottage," she whimpered
919 into her smock.
920   Unimpressed, the messenger
921 slumped down and sighed, "You
922 poor peasants! Have you no adequate
923 food at all?"
924   "As I told you, your Glory,"
925 came the sorrowful reply, "my father
926 has lost his mind and depends on me
927 to meet all his needs. There is only
928 so much a frail waif can accomplish
929 in an icy, lifeless world."
930   "I hope the KING will
931 understand why you can't serve
932 him," stuttered the messenger. Do
933 you know what he does to those who
934 rebuff him, even through no fault of
935 their own? Choose for yourself today
936 whom you will serve: your
937 Sovereign Lord or your unfortunate
938 circumstances."
939   The man leaned tentatively
940 toward the wispy girl and small
941 jewels of perspiration appeared on
942 her temple. But sweat appeared on
943 his brow as well, as he wondered
944 how the KING could possibly use
945 him in this particular situation.
946   Suddenly a tear appeared in one
947 of the girl's steel gray eyes. Then
948 another slipped down her pastel
949 cheek to alight on a tiny slippered
950 foot. "Your Holiness, truly I wish to
951 serve the King with all my heart, but

952 that is all I have to give—my poor,
953 broken, and unsuitable heart."
954   "Don't be sad, you poor spirit,"[51]
955 the messenger wheezed dejectedly.
956 "I can plainly see you have nothing
957 of worth to offer the KING.[52] No
958 special knowledge, talent or unique
959 qualities. No tea. He's coming
960 nevertheless. Perhaps I could offer
961 you to him as a scullery maid. You
962 know how to kneel and scrub steps, I
963 suppose, and light his candles when
964 it gets dark?"
965   With this the girl slipped into a
966 heap on the floor and began to sob
967 heavily, but silently. Surprisingly
968 though, she was soon able to pick
969 herself up and with a streaked face
970 look squarely into that of the
971 troubled messenger.
972   "Yes," she said evenly, "I am
973 able to scrub floors, but you will
974 never control my freedom of choice.
975 I am not your pampered poodle."
976   The messenger stared deeply
977 into her large, steady eyes. She held
978 him fixed until her determined gaze
979 sank deep and penetrated his melting
980 heart.

---

[51] Matthew 5: [3]Blessed are the poor in spirit, for theirs is the kingdom of heaven.

[52] Isaiah 64: [6]We have all become like one who is unclean, and all our righteous deeds are like a polluted garment. We all fade like a leaf, and our iniquities, like the wind, take us away.

981   "Small one," he asked, "why
982 should you devote your whole life to
983 a father who recognizes you not, and
984 thereby keeps you from your KING?
985 A KING who knows and loves you
986 better than anyone else knows and
987 loves you. Why would you thwart
988 his sovereign design? For hasn't he
989 stated his will that all should come to
990 him?[53] And isn't it written that all
991 who believe in him will be saved?"[54]

992   "Oh yes," came the answer, "but
993 I am not free to leave this place,
994 would that I could. The King would
995 not wish me to abandon my poor
996 beloved father, would he?"[55]

997   "But he has predestined it!" said
998 the messenger with an exasperated
999 look.

1000

1001   Just then outside there was a
1002 thundering through the forest and a
1003 wild galloping of horses, nostrils
1004 flaring, breaths puffing in great

---

[53] 1 Timothy 2: [3]This is good, and it is
pleasing in the sight of God our
Savior, [4]who desires all people to be saved
and to come to the knowledge of the truth.
[54] John 3: [16]"For God so loved the world,
that he gave his only Son, that whoever
believes in him should not perish but have
eternal life.
[55] Luke 14: [26]"If anyone comes to me and
does not hate his own father and mother and
wife and children and brothers and sisters,
yes, and even his own life, he cannot be my
disciple.

1005 steamy bellows. Snow from tree-
1006 branches, jarred loose by the
1007 commotion, descended in great
1008 clumps to the trail. Through them
1009 emerged the KING riding in radiant
1010 purple garments and under a great
1011 gilded riding-crown. He rode right
1012 up to the door of the cottage and
1013 stopped abruptly amidst a flurry of
1014 flowing cloaks. Immediately, the
1015 messenger rushed out to greet him on
1016 the snow laden landing.
1017   "Majesty," he said, bowing as
1018 low as possible while brandishing a
1019 feathered cap, "the poor soul inside,
1020 being confused in mind but resolute
1021 of heart is, heedless of my hard
1022 work, willfully refusing to accept
1023 Your Grace, even though you must
1024 have foreordained otherwise!
1025 Otherwise why would you have sent
1026 me here to have her prepare table?"
1027   The KING replied, "We
1028 predestine, but at the same time we
1029 confer complete and genuine choice.
1030 Alas both. We are in control; our
1031 favor, our grace, once bestowed is
1032 irresistible. Yet we do not force,
1033 coerce, or manipulate. For we are
1034 love and seek such love and worship
1035 in return.[56] We do not train puppies
1036 to jump through hoops. As a result

---

[56] 1 John 4: [16]So we have come to know and
to believe the love that God has for us. God
is love, and whoever abides in love abides in
God, and God abides in him.

37

1037 this girl is fully responsible for her
1038 actions and she will reap her just
1039 rewards."
1040   "Is that consistent?" the
1041 messenger dared to ask. "She is so
1042 sincere."
1043   "Consistent? Sincere? My ways
1044 and understandings are clearer than
1045 yours," said the KING, "for now, you
1046 search the pond bottom as if looking
1047 through winter ice. Later the spring
1048 will come."
1049   With this, the KING stroked his
1050 long beard and brushed snow out of
1051 it. For several moments he bowed his
1052 head as if lost in his own Kingly
1053 thoughts. "I think we should make
1054 some changes around here," he
1055 meditated. "I think we should shift
1056 some people around so everything
1057 can work out for good for those who
1058 love us, and are called according to
1059 our purpose."[57] So, with a hint of
1060 smile, he nodded knowingly and
1061 purposefully at the house, and then
1062 waited.
1063   After a few seconds, he turned
1064 his horse to depart, but called over
1065 his shoulder. "My graceful and dear
1066 novitiate," he said, "take these books
1067 and ride swiftly away to the next
1068 village. Arrange proper refreshment

---

[57] Romans 8: [28]And we know that for those
who love God all things work together for
good, for those who are called according to
his purpose.

1069 with someone. Someone I will show
1070 you. Make haste. Tell them the KING
1071 is coming."
1072
1073   From the window, and with the
1074 fire-glow burning bright behind, the
1075 black-clad man watched two figures
1076 depart down the snowy trail, then
1077 one ride swiftly ahead. This man in
1078 the window was the very same
1079 black-clad warrior who had the white
1080 collar and shiny, solid-silver belt
1081 buckle. His tall, black boots he had
1082 placed neatly by the door, and his
1083 gleaming sword he'd left in its
1084 scabbard on the horse. So with a sigh
1085 of relief, he began preparations to
1086 serve sassafras tea to the beloved
1087 papa who stared vacantly out the
1088 window. "After some nice head
1089 cheese,"[58] he beamed, "I shall begin
1090 reading to you from this wonderful
1091 new book your daughter gave me
1092 before she departed."[59]
1093   And as Faith rode ahead on her
1094 new silver steed, its mighty hooves
1095 churned up magnificent masses of
1096 dirt-flecked snow. The girl's cheeks
1097 began to glow and her blond hair

---

[58] Meat jelly of cooled, congealed stock
from boiling the cleaned out head of an
animal
[59] 2 Timothy 3: [16]All Scripture is breathed
out by God and profitable for teaching, for
reproof, for correction, and for training in
righteousness

1098 whipped furiously about her face,
1099 imparting a ruddy tint to the long
1100 locks. She rode effortlessly, but soon
1101 felt an irritating lump at her thigh. It
1102 was an old sword, which she
1103 immediately threw down, narrowly
1104 missing what looked like the head of
1105 a giant dragon, sleeping off a meal
1106 under the deep snow. "Away with
1107 you monster," she screamed into the
1108 wind.
1109   As soon as the sword tip hit the
1110 ground, the snow around it began to
1111 melt revealing fragile yellow-green
1112 grass underneath. And, lo and
1113 behold, this color spread ever
1114 outward like some fantastic ripple to
1115 paint a beautiful, emerald landscape
1116 of spring.
1117   "Here I am Lord, send me!"[60]
1118 the breathless girl cried, blinking
1119 back tears of joy. With all her might,
1120 in one hand she clutched the leather-
1121 sure reins of guidance and in the
1122 other, her leather-bound book of
1123 hope.
1124   "We must make haste," she
1125 whispered urgently into the horse's
1126 ear, "the KING is coming!"[61]

---

[60] Isaiah 6: [8]And I heard the voice of the
Lord saying, "Whom shall I send, and who
will go for us?" Then I said, "Here I am!
Send me."
[61] Revelation 19: [11]Then I saw heaven
opened, and behold, a white horse! The one
sitting on it is called Faithful and True, and

40

in righteousness he judges and makes war. [12]His eyes are like a flame of fire, and on his head are many diadems, and he has a name written that no one knows but himself. [13]He is clothed in a robe dipped in blood, and the name by which he is called is The Word of God. [14]And the armies of heaven, arrayed in fine linen, white and pure, were following him on white horses. [15]From his mouth comes a sharp sword with which to strike down the nations, and he will rule them with a rod of iron. He will tread the winepress of the fury of the wrath of God the Almighty. [16]On his robe and on his thigh he has a name written, King of kings and Lord of lords.

[17]Then I saw an angel standing in the sun, and with a loud voice he called to all the birds that fly directly overhead, "Come, gather for the great supper of God, [18]to eat the flesh of kings, the flesh of captains, the flesh of mighty men, the flesh of horses and their riders, and the flesh of all men, both free and slave, both small and great." [19]And I saw the beast and the kings of the earth with their armies gathered to make war against him who was sitting on the horse and against his army. [20]And the beast was captured, and with it the false prophet who in its presence had done the signs by which he deceived those who had received the mark of the beast and those who worshiped its image. These two were thrown alive into the lake of fire that burns with sulfur. [21]And the rest were slain by the sword that came from the mouth of him who was sitting on the horse, and all the birds were gorged with their flesh.

Epilogue

1   A few years passed and the
2 KING had reportedly returned to his
3 castle. With all the rumors nobody
4 knew what to believe anymore.
5 Many who purported to know the
6 Sovereign well, knew only what they
7 fancied about him—not even
8 bothering to properly read his book.
9 Most of them relegated the KING to
10 the role of imaginary helper, and
11 then only in times of trouble.
12   In any event, the countryside
13 had grown white and cold again. The
14 rivers froze dead with ugly sticks
15 protruding like spears. Oaks clung
16 desperately to brown, lifeless leaves
17 as other trees leaned naked, weary
18 against a gray sky. Butterflies
19 expired and shriveled. Rime ice
20 turned reeds and willows into broken
21 latticework while evergreen boughs
22 bowed low under landscapes of
23 snow. Snow lay oppressive
24 everywhere. A foul wind clutched
25 loose clumps and plastered them
26 white against tree trunks. The dragon
27 was still lapping at many doors, even
28 as the KING'S messengers knocked
29 on others. The dragon marked his
30 doors as a dog would; the KING
31 marked his own with his very own
32 blood.[62] War was brewing. A war, to

33 be sure, which continues to this very
34 day. Battle lines have been drawn.
35 By the way, those of us who aren't
36 with the KING in this fight are
37 counted as against him.[63] Sobering
38 news. Are you awake?
39
40   The black-clad soldier continued
41 living in Honeysuckle Haven and
42 ministered daily to Faith's father.
43 Everyone began to call him
44 Abraham.[64] The old man's only joy
45 seemed to flow from following the
46 Book of Books, which was read to
47 him daily. At times there could be
48 seen an ever-so-subtle glimmer in
49 the eye, an almost imperceptible
50 glow of the cheek, a hint of grin at a

---

[62] Exodus 12: [21]Then Moses called all the
elders of Israel and said to them, "Go and
select lambs for yourselves according to
your clans, and kill the Passover
lamb. [22]Take a bunch of hyssop and dip it in
the blood that is in the basin, and touch the
lintel and the two doorposts with the blood
that is in the basin. None of you shall go out
of the door of his house until the
morning. [23]For the LORD will pass through
to strike the Egyptians, and when he sees the
blood on the lintel and on the two doorposts,
the LORD will pass over the door and will
not allow the destroyer to enter your houses
to strike you.
[63] Matthew 12: [30]Whoever is not with me is
against me, and whoever does not gather
with me scatters.
[64] Galatians 3: [7]Know then that it is those of
faith who are the sons of Abraham.

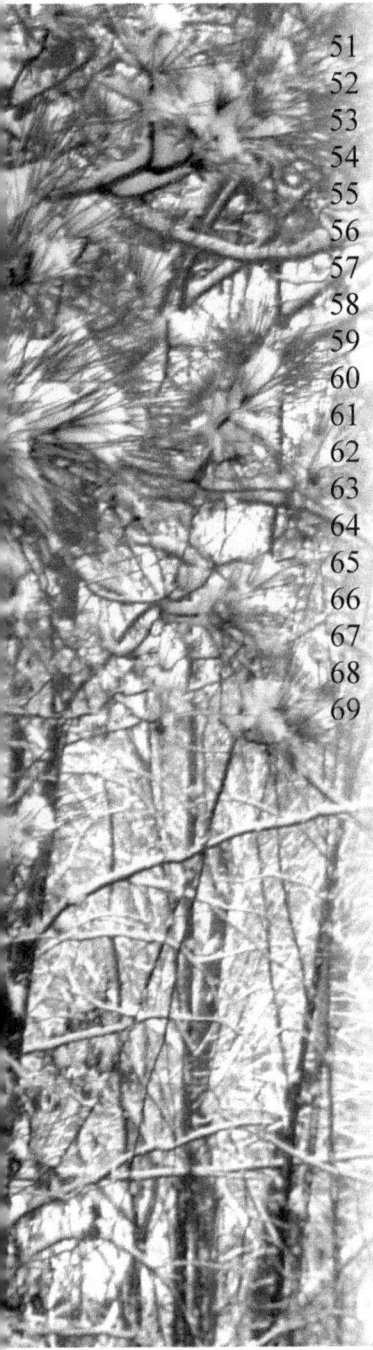

51 mouth corner—fleeting and faint.
52 But false? One had to wonder.
53   Also the soldier, not
54 surprisingly, was strongly affected
55 by these readings. Influenced to the
56 extent that it broke his pride and he
57 recognized the KING as his real and
58 true Master-Lord. Yes, heretofore he
59 had been outwardly the High-KING'S
60 messenger—without actually being
61 part of his kingdom at all![65] The
62 pages of love now began to unfold
63 before him, not as myth or mere
64 philosophy, but as living Word.[66] It
65 convincingly and convictingly made
66 claims on his heart and mind. It
67 changed him.
68   Of course, the mindless father
69 Abraham could make no such

---

[65] Matthew 7: [22]On that day many will say to me, 'Lord, Lord, did we not prophesy in your name, and cast out demons in your name, and do many mighty works in your name?' [23]And then will I declare to them, 'I never knew you; depart from me, you workers of lawlessness.'

[66] John 1: [1]In the beginning was the Word, and the Word was with God, and the Word was God. [2]He was in the beginning with God. [3]All things were made through him, and without him was not any thing made that was made. [4]In him was life, and the life was the light of men. [5]The light shines in the darkness, and the darkness has not overcome it. [14]And the Word became flesh and dwelt among us, and we have seen his glory, glory as of the only Son from the Father, full of grace and truth.

70 profession of faith, either outwardly
71 or inwardly. Or could he? He often
72 stared out the window at birds. Did
73 he reflect on their creator and
74 sustainer?[67] He seemed comforted by
75 the reading of Scripture. Did he ever
76 consider its author and illuminator?[68]
77 Maybe such things are not for earthly
78 stewards to know. Yet the KING
79 would know.
80
81   One particularly bright day the
82 soldier spotted an unusual point of
83 reflection in the snow. It was some
84 distance down the trail. Curious, he
85 donned his boots and coat and
86 trudged out to it. It turned out to be
87 his old sword, carelessly discarded
88 and stuck in the frozen wayside mud.
89 Naturally he was unable to pull it
90 out, and too much tugging and
91 bending would certainly break it. He
92 could wait for spring—but of late,
93 spring was never coming to this
94 particular countryside. So he took
95 great pains to scoop away snow, chip
96 at the ice, and build a fire around
97 it—all this without actually touching
98 the sword itself. In spite of these
99 elaborate and time consuming efforts

---

[67] Colossians 1: [17]And he is before all things, and in him all things hold together.
[68] John 14: [26]But the Helper, the Holy Spirit, whom the Father will send in my name, he will teach you all things and bring to your remembrance all that I have said to you.

100   he was unable to extract it. Almost as
101   an afterthought he decided to pray.[69]
102   Straight away the weapon became an
103   attractive, if superfluous ornament
104   above his mantel piece.
105   Yet in short order it would prove
106   not so entirely useless after all. You
107   see, like I said before, the dragon
108   was licking at many doors, lusting
109   after unprotected morsels. Are you
110   still awake?
111
112   As the beast was approaching
113   Honeysuckle Haven, he sensed a
114   presence not often found throughout
115   the countryside. It was the Spirit of
116   the KING, and his force was strong.
117   Nevertheless the dragon rose up to
118   its full height and scratched on the
119   door with something menacing that
120   resembled a raptor claw.
121   This time it was not a little girl
122   who answered but a brave, sword-
123   carrying warrior in full armor.[70]

---

[69] John 16: [24]Until now you have asked
nothing in my name. Ask, and you will
receive, that your joy may be full.
[70] Ephesians 6: [10]Finally, be strong in the
Lord and in the strength of his might. [11]Put
on the whole armor of God, that you may be
able to stand against the schemes of the
devil. [12]For we do not wrestle against flesh
and blood, but against the rulers, against the
authorities, against the cosmic powers over
this present darkness, against the spiritual
forces of evil in the heavenly
places. [13]Therefore take up the whole armor

124 "Would you have but a crust of
125 bread for a poor, starving newt?" the
126 dragon asked, trying to blink
127 sheepishly.
128 "You look rather large for a
129 newt," the man replied.
130 "I am Sir Newt Rocknee, Knight
131 Lord of Michael and Saint George,
132 KLMG" said the dragon, puffing out
133 his chest.
134 "Night lord of the flies,[71] your
135 heinous," the soldier mocked.
136 At that moment the dragon
137 noticed a figure hunched over in the
138 next room—staring blankly into a
139 corner. Hmmm. Plenty of delicious
140 fresh flesh without a keen mind to
141 defend it.
142 "Away with you," the soldier
143 brandished his sword, "the KING
144 says you are already defeated."[72]

---

of God, that you may be able to withstand in the evil day, and having done all, to stand firm. [14]Stand therefore, having fastened on the belt of truth, and having put on the breastplate of righteousness, [15]and, as shoes for your feet, having put on the readiness given by the gospel of peace. [16]In all circumstances take up the shield of faith, with which you can extinguish all the flaming darts of the evil one; [17]and take the helmet of salvation, and the sword of the Spirit, which is the word of God, [18]praying at all times in the Spirit, with all prayer and supplication. To that end keep alert with all perseverance, making supplication for all the saints

[71] Beelzebul

145   "The king is a liar."[73] The words
146 stuck in the dragon's throat like a
147 death rattle. With a growl he lunged
148 forward, breaking the door hinges
149 and sweeping the sword aside. The
150 two grappled and fell hard to the
151 floor. The man's armor protected
152 him from the dagger-like teeth, but it
153 was hard to avoid dragon scratches.
154 There was so much scuffling, huffing
155 and puffing, the drapes caught fire.
156 Curious how so much hot smoke and
157 fire could come out of one cold-
158 bodied lizard.
159   The man was finding that, while
160 the KING'S Armor was durable
161 enough, his weak use of it was
162 draining. The dragon was pure evil
163 and more powerful than any man,
164 beast or angel.[74] The battle was not
165 going well.

---

[72] Revelation 20: [10]and the devil who had deceived them was thrown into the lake of fire and sulfur where the beast and the false prophet were, and they will be tormented day and night forever and ever.

[73] John 8: [44]You are of your father the devil, and your will is to do your father's desires. He was a murderer from the beginning, and does not stand in the truth, because there is no truth in him. When he lies, he speaks out of his own character, for he is a liar and the father of lies.

[74] Jude 1: [9]But when the archangel Michael, contending with the devil, was disputing about the body of Moses, he did not presume to pronounce a blasphemous judgment, but said, "The Lord rebuke you."

166
167   Just then Faith, the fair daughter
168 of Abraham, resplendent in white
169 robes and silver armor pulled up on
170 her mighty horse. Her sword was
171 long, sure and two-edged. At her
172 thigh she carried the leather-bound
173 book that was her only guide.
174   And she was not alone. She led
175 a battalion of new KING-believers,
176 similarly equipped and all keen for
177 battle. Every one of them had
178 pledged undying allegiance not to
179 her, but to their KING-Lord and
180 Master. Since they could not all fit
181 into the tiny shack, they tossed water
182 on the flaming drapes and dragged
183 the smoldering dragon out to
184 continue the battle on the front lawn.
185 It was the only patch of green for
186 miles—but it was rapidly turning
187 crimson.
188   Unfortunately, thousands of
189 poisonous spit-lizards heard the
190 reptilian screams and quickly
191 materialized from dark dimensions to
192 join the fray. They could strike from
193 any distance and cause blinding pain
194 to the eyes.[75] With them came hordes
195 of malicious human militia. They
196 came from slums, shantytowns, in

---

[75] 2 Corinthians 4: [4]In their case the god of
this world has blinded the minds of the
unbelievers, to keep them from seeing the
light of the gospel of the glory of Christ,
who is the image of God.

197 packs like wolves[76] and armed with
198 assault bows. Dissatisfied with the
199 KING, they called themselves
200 'Citizens,' and the forces of Faith
201 they referred to as 'Monarchists.'
202 Again the tide of battle turned
203 against the soldiers of the KING.
204   The battle spread far and wide
205 with all manner of carnage and death
206 coming to combatant and civilian
207 alike—guilty and innocent alike.
208 Children were slain. Even babies.
209 Sometimes on purpose. Soon it
210 became difficult, then impossible to
211 bury all the dead. Blood did actually
212 flow like rivers. Citizen blood
213 mingled grotesquely with
214 Monarchist. Human with reptilian.
215 Warm with cold. Countless mothers
216 would later search in vain for their
217 fallen battle-sons and weep at mock
218 funerals. To maintain their slipping
219 sanity they would spin brokenhearted
220 tales of fanciful heroism, fantasized
221 salvation prayers, and peaceful death
222 fabrications. True or false, they had
223 to believe that all departed sons were
224 now in blissful repose.
225   Then just before all seemed lost,
226 the KING himself appeared.

---

[76] Acts 20: [29] I know that after my departure fierce wolves will come in among you, not sparing the flock; [30] and from among your own selves will arise men speaking twisted things, to draw away the disciples after them.

227   Oh such a spectacle it would
228 have been to see our KING in action
229 with his righteous right hand[77] and
230 terrible swift sword.[78] Such
231 satisfaction to see villains slashed,
232 their heads rolling in gullies. How
233 liberating to walk over evil bodies
234 crushed and pulverized. But alas, no.
235 The KING vanquished them with just
236 one word:[79]
237
238 **"Damnation!"**
239
240   This caused all fighting to stop
241 and the despicable reptiles hung their
242 heads like naughty puppies. Soon
243 they began whining and begging for
244 mercy. As the KING glared at them
245 they began slinking away, licking
246 their wounds, and dragging their
247 dung encrusted tails in the dirt. Their
248 time for final judgment had yet to
249 come. The 'Citizens,' squinting
250 sideways at each other, melted back
251 into the countryside. From behind

---

[77] Isaiah 41: [10]fear not, for I am with you; be not dismayed, for I am your God; I will strengthen you, I will help you, I will uphold you with my righteous right hand.
[78] a phrase from "The Battle Hymn of the Republic" by Julia Ward Howe
[79] Hebrews 4: [12]For the word of God is living and active, sharper than any two-edged sword, piercing to the division of soul and of spirit, of joints and of marrow, and discerning the thoughts and intentions of the heart.

252 bushes they murmured accusations
253 of hate crimes against the KING and
254 other blasphemies.[80]
255
256　　　As for the 'Monarchists,'
257 immediately there was great
258 rejoicing around the KING, which
259 rapidly turned into worship and
260 complete adoration as he reached out
261 to heal many of the wounded.[81] The
262 landscape grew brighter and pulsated
263 with color. There was singing and
264 ringing of bells—a general overflow
265 of merriment. Many tears of joy as
266 well, even from iron-jawed men and
267 steely-eyed women.
268　　　In due time however, they all
269 headed back toward the castle. First
270 stop on the trail, a return to Stoutnest
271 Manor. This was where the KING'S
272 messenger had encountered Hope,
273 the second young maiden. They
274 wondered what they would find now.
275 Would there be a book being read by
276 a young girl? One retrieved from a
277 cabinet? One could hope. One could
278 pray.
279

---

[80] Psalm 106: [25]They murmured in their tents, and did not obey the voice of the Lord.
[81] Acts 10: [38]how God anointed Jesus of Nazareth with the Holy Spirit and with power. He went about doing good and healing all who were oppressed by the devil, for God was with him.

280　　　　But Faith lingered behind. She
281　searched frantically about until
282　eventually she found her dear father
283　huddling in a small closet where
284　someone must have placed him for
285　safekeeping. He was pale. He was
286　bent over. He was trembling. She
287　hugged him, gave him a kiss—wiped
288　away his tear. Would he be coming
289　with them to the castle? Was there a
290　room prepared for him?[82] Was his
291　name written in the Book of Life?[83]
292　She looked deeply into his ancient
293　eyes. They looked moist, sweet, but
294　vacant. He didn't recognize her. She
295　started to cry.
296　　　　But just then the KING doubled
297　back and burst into the house.
298　"Abraham!" he called, and swept the
299　old man up with him onto the back
300　of his horse.
301　　　　"Hurry up, small Faith," he
302　called back, "don't be left behind.
303　The KING is heading home.

---

[82] John 14: [2]In my Father's house are many
rooms. If it were not so, would I have told
you that I go to prepare a place for you?
[83] Revelation 20: [15]And if anyone's name
was not found written in the book of life, he
was thrown into the lake of fire.